Libation

Earl Livings was born and educated in Melbourne, Australia. On his way to a career in writing, he played guitar in a garage band, gained a black belt in kung fu, studied theoretical physics, and worked as a statistician, a productivity manager in a factory, and a university administrator. He taught professional writing and editing for almost twenty years and was the editor of *Divan*, Australia's first all-Australian online poetry journal, from 1999 to 2013. His poetry and fiction have been published in journals and anthologies in Australia, and also in Britain, Canada, the USA and Germany. Earl's first poetry collection, *Further than Night* (Bystander Press), was published in 2000, and in 2005 he won the Melbourne Poets Union International Poetry Competition. Earl lives in Melbourne with his wife, Jo, and is currently working on a Dark Ages novel and his next poetry collection.

Earl Livings

Libation

For my children, Chad, Kelly, Robert and Patrick

Libation
ISBN 978 1 76041 615 7
Copyright © text Earl Livings 2018
Cover photo: Earl Livings

First published 2018 by
GINNINDERRA PRESS
PO Box 3461 Port Adelaide 5015
www.ginninderrapress.com.au

Contents

Libation	9
Cleave	11
Notions	12
Experiment with Soul	13
Totems	14
Tawny Frogmouth	15
The Silence of the Daguerreotype	16
Alien Dispatch	18
Music for Nothing	21
Further Propositions on the End of the Universe	23
Down Below	26
Face to Face	27
Fall Out	28
Easeful Death	30
Bardo for Mother and Son	32
The Orchids and My Father	33
Portrait in 4D	34
Black, with One White Spot	36
Venture	37
Man and Hunt	38
We Survivors	39
Initiation	40
Dolmen and Circle	41
Newgrange Return	43
Scripture in the Round	44
Wu-Wei	45
Letter to William Blake	47
Climbing Glastonbury Tor	48
Weft	50
Design: Mt Ngungun	51

Looking for Grace	53
The Dream Bird	54
Homecoming	55
Above, Below	57
Contact	59
This Enterprise of Dust	60
Palette	61
How We Come to Touch	62
Lemniscate	64
This Charge Between Us	65
Spanish Bluebells	66
Moments after Meditation	67
Naming Instinct	68
Summer Adepts	70
Little Wattlebird	72
Climbing the Tree	74
Kondalilla Falls	76
The Decree of All Dreams	79
Summer Walk, Early	81
Acknowledgements	82

'As a man is, so he sees. As the Eye is formed, such are its Powers.'

William Blake, 'Letter to the Rev Dr. Trusler, August 23, 1799'

Libation

To the earth my ancestors
Offered the best or the first –
Hindquarter, sheaf of wheat, blood –
Respect for those spirits felt
In tree, stream, stone, mystery:
How and why sun and moon dance,
How creatures and crops follow
The seasons, where the dead go.

In my childhood, taught and blessed
By revelation dogma,
I gave thanks to that one god
I soon judged didn't exist,
The bounty at our table
Not his to bestow, but ours –
The marvel of jump-stump ploughs,
The charge of superphosphates,
The chain gears in abattoirs –
Man's inventions helping man.

This full-moon night I open
A bottle of Welsh whisky,
Pour some on the rooted earth
Of our apple tree, listen
To the wind jostle the leaves
Of my thoughts. I have watched man
Land on the moon and track signs
For alpha and omega
In the folds of particles
And the spiral attractions

Of galaxies, flowers, shells.
Have heard reasons for murder
In common streets, holy sites,
The control of hierarchies.
Have felt the chaos designs
Of weather and human touch.

Though I can never be sure
Of anything, life itself
A mask out of mystery,
I have once or twice found grace
In meditation and out
Of the corner of an eye,
In forest, at seashore,
With lover or newborn,
A scintillation, a keen trace,
Unplucked string resonating
To a distant rare music,
One part ceremony, one part dance,
Presence that encourages
And deserves honour, some chance
For alliance – planet, self,
Winds that rattle, disappear.

Cleave

The boy rests on the soft slope watching stars entice him, incite him. Hands folded behind his head, he hears the insistent buzz of insects as they hunt, are hunted. One Doppler-dives towards him. He does not move, does not change his breathing as it flies near, brief interruption of light from a distant sun. He watches the sky, his thoughts. Sometimes thought fades as eyes close and breathing slows. Then call of night bird or screech of insect flight brings him to the moment, and he studies the cloudless, sharp and cyclic night.

How often has he dreamed the touch of stars? How often has he reached out to touch the wind that touches the sky that touches dreams under other skies? How often will scent of flower or lover open memory and kindle him with all things he desires, moon, sun and stars within him?

When he shuts his eyes once more on sign and omen, he welcomes darkness inside, blaze of life toiling about him, shadow of his life tracking shadows of all lives.

Knows that to burn brightly casts no shadow, burns away shadows.

Craves the hottest flame, which always works unseen.

Notions

Pluralitas non est ponenda sine necessitate
Plurality should not be posited without necessity
– William of Ockham

In my first serious essay
For Religious Studies
I apply Occam's razor
(Choice of budding scientist)
To God's reputation:
All power to do all things,
All essence in all things,
All guidance for all things,
Past, present, future.

Keeping it simple, I favour
The universe as is, in its cycles
Of bloom and dust, orbits
And double-helix feats, all
Loosed by laws of urge
And reaction, lure and strife,
First seed, last song,
Billiard balls colliding
Ad infinitum, no recourse
To maker or judge.

I await appreciation
Of insight and logic, but
None comes, others praised
In a covenant of dogma,
My first taste of discourse
By dismissal, my first vow
For the vigour of heresy.

Experiment with Soul

In science one day he tried
To weigh his soul, the Devil
On one shoulder, an angel
On the other – to believe
Either meant soul 'must' exist,
So the books and priests said.
But how to separate it
From his body? Where was it?
In his welts and tears when struck
By a bully, upset parent.
In his erection at night
Or during lessons after
Seeing high skirts on the train.
In the charge that twitched frogs' legs.
In the incense and his prayers
At Mass. In those eyes looking
Out from the mirror, gold flakes
In brown iris, flash of light
Deep in the swollen pupils…

Nightly he stares through the stars,
Patterns flickering in-out
Of focus and naming, feels
Grave darkness open around
And inside him, falls towards
That one whisper he can trust,
Distant roar, wind and burning.

Totems

'The body has its secrets and mysteries, memories and visions'
– Susan Browne

In my cells, now, fish, flesh, fowl –
All creatures blessed, hunted, tamed,
Blossoming epochs of life
Scavenging any fit niche,
Memory of those extinct
By ill luck or our own hand,
And those watched or imagined
When we were just a tree shrew
Or erecting monuments
To achievement and control,
Gods, demons, heroes, monsters,
In painting, stone, text and song,
Jackal-headed judge, cloven-
Hoofed drunken dancer, lion-
Bodied, eagle-winged, serpent-
Tailed keeper of emerald
Knowledge – tomb, grail, tree of life,
Tadpole and fish in the womb,
The spine's crimson claw and snarl,

Each moment's constellation
Of lust, flight, fight enflaming
Each cell, pounding at reason,
Duty, language, the salmon
Thrusting upstream, the panther
Pouncing and tearing at prey,

The owl staring out my eyes.

Tawny Frogmouth

Stunned by this sudden cave
Of glass, metal gadgets, straight edges,
The floored bird swivel-head stares
At our locked gaze, hunches so still
I think oven mitts unnecessary
For capture. We breathe together.

Its wildness springs into flight.
Wings flail the ceiling, that sound
Like books falling from shelves.
The bird shudder-drops, lands
With its amber-bulb eyes inches
From the doorjamb. We coo and shoo.

It hops sideways, senses the wide
Dark beyond the door we opened
For cool breezes, dark rectangle
In the dark house it did not see
But may remember. Spreads itself
To the night, the lure of home.

Lifts itself on a single beat.
Rises swiftly towards distant trees.
We stare at each other, the wonder
Of wildness so easily trapped, gone,
Close the door, turn off the lights,
Listen to the silence, to our longing.

The Silence of the Daguerreotype

Boulevard du Temple, Paris, Spring 1838

A man opens the shutter
Of his apparatus, waits
Fifteen minutes for the crests
And dips of light to tarnish
The layer of iodised
Silver on its copper plate,
So that mercury vapour
And a solution of salt
Can draw out a mirror world,
The real one now history:

A divided road, traffic
Too swift for capture, buildings,
Chimney pots, sun-blurred shadows,
Wind-fuzzy trees, and a man,
Foot raised for the shoeshine boy,
A man reading the paper,
A man under the awning
Of a tavern, a woman
Next to a lamp post, maybe
Watching the first man, and in
The big white building nearby
An old woman studying
The to and fro of the street,
While two storeys up, a child
Peers through curtains to where
The contraption watches him…

These the first people ever
Photographed – their rough likeness,
What attracts them, forever
Fixed, stored in a glass case filled
With nitrogen gas to stop
Something more than memory,
Or less, from fading before
Re-exposing us to us…

Who stand or sit long enough
To study those shining eyes
In the polish of our shoes,
Talk to any old stranger
Smiling with a steady lens,
Sigh into that found silence.

Alien Dispatch

'It is possible that the future of human civilization depends on the receipt of interstellar messages' – Carl Sagan

I'm not supposed to know your name.
There are yet worlds where speech
Has consequence, as once here
When words spoken by chance
Would spill honey from ears,
Spin wind through eyes,
Freeze all consideration of breath.
So, let's just call ourselves
By the same name, and we will be
No longer strangers, our power only
Over each other's compact of words.

Again cicadas are applauding nightfall –
A million miniature bone plates clattering
(There is so much we assume translates)

And children are laughing
Into lures of darkness,
Shredding the call of mothers.

What are you doing this moment?
(I assume there is time, assume too
Such integrity of senses
Silence has its correspondence.)

Hoping for my first star tonight,
A pantheon of faith, I look up,
See house lights and my locked face
Transcribing my window.

Dare we go into that under-dark
Where there are no visions
But what we imagine?
Tell me about your dreams.
Someone here experimented
With dream deprivation.
They all went mad, of course.
I hope you're not mad too,
Then you may not write me.

Still giggling, the children have gone
To their mothers. And you?

Have you ever seen a kestrel
Hover like a pause that gently
Tugs the breath in your cheeks,
And then,
Hugging its hunger to itself,
Plummet upon a coursing shadow?
Dare we sigh after such moments?
Is one common bond a need for surprise?

Stars and dreams of touching
Unravel necessary delusions.
Are there always clouds above you,
Or do you live deep in caves
Where light does not flicker
Or true shadows entice?
Under the earth is another dream.

How many names for love have you?
For death? Are they the same?
What is your death may not be mine.
What is love but an unlocked mask?

Always we send out these questions
And hope, at least, for one answer.
Were they the right questions?

One day stars may gasp
For a moment, decline all shadows.
Maybe it's only right
To ask questions without answers.
Are they the right questions?
Maybe words are the merest flicker
Of questions we must always ask.
Maybe dreams rejoin the dark…

It is morning now and this world
Is one million letters for raindrops.
Keen as light through barred sky
A bird traverses my window.
A child is shouting in the wind.
Is that its first question?
Moments ago there were no smiles.

Write soon.

Music for Nothing

Imagine this: the bass note
Of the Big Bang dropping deeper
Into its own hollow rumble
As the universe expands forever,
Dark energy the engine of repulsion
Against mutual attraction
Of time, space, their interstices
Of ordinary mass: our bodies,
What we breathe, what we stand on,
What we consume, what consumes us,
Those long negotiations of nurture,
Billowing artefacts of thought.

Imagine it: the note drops while stars
Run out of fuel, cool into supernovae
Which scatter their baked elements
Into new clottings of star systems,
Till distance defuses gravitational lures,
Fuel fizzles, the wick of light splutters,
Planets plunge into the maws of suns
Swelling before their final collapse
Or whirl from orbit like stones from slings,

Life scrambling from world to world
Till nothing remains of breath
But inscriptions on rock, metal,
The quantum waves of particles,
To fade, crumble, dissolve,

Even the last tyrant's whim
Of star cluster name and title
Drifting apart long after anyone
Survives to read and shiver,
All known no longer known,
Imperative to life corrupted
By cosmic entropy, grey
Skim of absolute motion
Drawn thinner than prayer,
More stilled than rapture,

Long after the last black hole
Winks its frayed horizon,
A balloon swallowing itself.

Now imagine nothing, the final
Still note, the total absence
Of anything, the dreamless
Abyss, the borderless gap
Within gaps, nothing as lack
Of presence and absence, itself
A something that is not itself,
Nothing, then that echo of solitude,
A grace note somewhat like a gathering
Of all intellect and care into one
Kindling flourish of nothing,
A seed note surging awe and lush shapes.
Just imagine it, now, or soon enough.

Further Propositions on the End of the Universe

1

God said, 'That's enough,'
And pinched Himself awake.

2

God does not exist.
Those who believe He does
Killed those who don't,
Or vice versa,
And entropy took care of the rest.

3

Each universe is one of a pair,
Like virtual particles,
And they annihilate each other.

4

There is no universe.

5

At the end of the universe is a black hole.
In the middle of the black hole is a white hole.
In the middle of the white hole is another black hole,
Or God, or the Goddess,
Or maybe just a science fiction writer.

6

There are no science fiction writers,
Only apprentice gods and goddesses.

7

The ship at the end of the universe
Opens a portal to the one next to it,
Finds itself back in the old one,
Rides the shock wave of the Big Bang,
Leaves a message in the background radiation.

8

The ship at the end of the universe
Finds an open portal,
Collides with a ship coming the other way.

9

God is an unpublished science fiction writer.

10

The universe is a dream
Dreamt by another universe,
Ad infinitum.

11

Who cares what happens to the universe?
I won't be there.

12

If I am there,
I had a great time getting there.

13

Some sleeping god blinks,
And a universe like the first one,
Or completely unlike it,
Comes into being.

14

At the end of the universe
Life has evolved to cosmic consciousness,
And its laughter creates a new one.

15

The universe is a Möbius strip.

16

Two universes combine to make a third one,
Ad infinitum.

17

The number of universes is an ever-growing prime number.

18

If a universe did not exist
Nothingness would invent one.

Down Below

You smear spittle across the inside of your face mask
To prevent it fogging, watch the serrated edge of air
And sea refract the dive-line as if to say
Nothing here is ever straight.

You plunge, water smothering sound, shunting
The reflex cold of light disappearing behind you,
Haul yourself down a narrowing cone of thought
As depth pressures lung, eardrum, eyeball,
As motes of sea sway out of vision,
Darkness deepening to the point.

You turn towards the flickering iris of sense
Above you, the blowhole of your snorkel
Goading you to breathe, wonder what remains
In that reflected cone, where each inch of depth
Compresses light and movement,
That ebony of flooded eyes.

Somewhere past the spotlight of any deep craft
Scripting wonders for Discovery Channel,
Undulating membranes flatten nerves, eyes
Across the sweep of gloom, weight above
Equal to that below, would cling to legs
If you could kick, would drag you
Deeper, wider, if you could see.

Face to Face

Death is not my true name,
Nor the nature of my work.
That decay you sniff

Is your second-last breath
Laced with effluence
Of organ meltdown.

That sound, twitch of artery,
Prayer in last gasp,
Rasp of eyelids closing.

That touch, quick jading
Of nerves cragged by light.
That taste, minerals

Recycling into carbon grace.
And what you see as eyes
Roll back on time

Is that mirror of silence
At the back of your mind –
How it braids the shadows

Behind each venture
Flung aside, each setback.
How it summons the yearning

That once kindled your face.
How it cheers the birth
Of all work we puzzle together.

Fall Out

Dead now thirty years or more, you were
Just one of the neighbourhood knockabout kids
Kicking a rolled-up-newspaper-and-twine footy,
Racing bikes and billycarts down the hill,
Playing gangs in the paddock across the road
With its grass-hillock hideaways, rubbish-mound forts,
Whooping and hooting with the next fruit box tossed
Flinting sparks and flames on the Guy Fawkes bonfire,
Skyrockets whoosh-slicing the night to the refrain
Of bolts and penny bangers in metal pipes.

Once, in the dust-gloom under my home,
Housing Commission brick-veneer own-your-own,
We played Nazi Europe with my new toy soldiers –
Battlefield machismo and glory, tactics and blunders,
The ricochet of machine gun and death rattle,
Trench and bunker, blitzkrieg and hand-to-hand combat –
Till night forced toy troops into their foxholes
And us generals to meat-and-three-veg meals,
Supervised TV after chores and homework (at least
At our place), torchlight reading under bedclothes.
After school the next day, the toys were not R & R
In some misplaced barrack under the house,
But AWOL, the trial of betrayal confined
To my parents' advice: 'You're better off…'

Maybe I was, given the growing distinctions:
State education versus Catholic schools;
Fumblings with girls near the creek at lunchtime
Versus chaperoned formals; swagger of stovepipes,
Sideburns and cigarettes versus books under the arm
And four-eyes glued to lecture room blackboards.
We moved to a bigger house, more prudent suburb,
Heard little of your exploits, whether social
Or petty criminal, then that night, drunk,
Outside the pub, a bet that you could show 'em
How to stop the next car with your body,
The bet won, your right leg amputated.
Crutches were your medals of bravado.
Then another car stopped you: your girlfriend
And her lover chasing you down a gravel road,
Running you over again just to make sure,
Suburb and description on the news, no name.

Whenever I have recalled you since,
It's the fraught terror of your triple-limb flight,
The disbelief at savagery of spinning wheels,
Splintered wood, dust and blood. And now
Your hobbling appearance last night
In a dream of dirt, smoky darkness,
Rows of house stumps like mausoleum columns,
The bolt-upright clue of a handful of lead soldiers
In your coat pocket, your face always in shade.

Easeful Death

The Keats Room, Keats-Shelley House, Piazza di Spagna, Rome, October 2007

The truth is, only his death mask yields beauty.
Everything else in the poet's sickroom is replica,
Except the fireplace where his friend Joseph Severn
Warmed his food, till milk was all Keats could have
On his better days – when not coughing up blood
And mucus, when bloodletting and starvation diets
Brought mixed relief, when he could think on
Fanny Brawne and suffer the dazzle-spear
That always went through him. After his death
The authorities burned linen, clothing, curtains
And bed, even the wallpaper, in the street outside.

Griefed by failure and love, he died of consumption,
Like his mother and brother, at less than half
My present age. At least some critics praised
His third book – those vigorous odes, written before
The final warrant of blood-vomit and palpitations –
Yet he was too far from walks upon Hampstead Heath
With friends, too far from family, from England, too far
Into haemorrhages of mind and body for such news
And the mild climate of Rome to save him.
From his bed he could hear the crowds bustling
Up and down the *Scalinata*, those cataract steps
Outside his window, could hear the lapping
Of Bernini's *Barcaccia*, the galley fountain
At the bottom of the steps, could hear
On his better days the fret of death.

Above his epitaph, Severn placed the symbol
Of a broken lyre. Fanny's unopened letters
And a lock of her hair were buried with him.
Violets, his favourite, overspread his grave.

Bardo for Mother and Son

'I think of a bardo as being like a moment when you step to the edge of a precipice…' – Sogyal Rinpoche, *The Tibetan Book of Living and Dying*

Last night I dreamed coming home
From school, not the usual direction,
Saw you peering from my bedroom window,
Saw the young burglars you'd scared off.
I gave chase, caught them, scolded them,
Returned to the house you loved,
Though here, with too many windows,
Though here, shaded by large deciduous trees,
And your bedroom displayed more
Religious paraphernalia than ever we had,
Strange communion of bardo and loss.
When the thieves' father came to threaten us
I fought him like the man I would become,
While you dialled the priest instead of police,
A black Bakelite phone we never had.

Your journey and mine diverged
Many times – death is the latest –
With more dreams, more encounters,
More chance illumination

Like when I walked home
To save the bus fare
And you asked if I liked my icy-pole –
'A little birdie told me,' you said –
The coloured stain around my lips
A dead giveaway.

The Orchids and My Father

'The map is not the territory' – Alfred Korzybski

After the procedure he lies flat
On his hospital bed and, as we often do,
We dismember theory and fact, today's task
Western culture's bias for abstractions,
Reality just beyond the corners of words.

He tells me how hard it is to tell others
Of his childhood spent in Karri forests,
How you can walk fifty yards and not see
The road – no underbrush, only more trees,
The sun a green haze all about you.

Hardest to explain is the sudden field
Of orchids – its dazzle-mass of colours –
Or that time a Japanese soldier
Rose from jungle grass before him
'Hand-to-hand… Either him or me.'

Portrait in 4D

Picturing things in four dimensions –
Gears, shafts, sprockets, chains,
All sizes, shapes, thicknesses interlocked,
Pushing, pulling, spinning every direction,
Forces harnessed into useful work –
This was my father's claim to imagination.

Not the fantasy realms of my youth –
Gryphons, shapeshifters, magic rings,
Heroes with radioactive powers,
Warfare of men with gods, with aliens –
Though he did read some science fiction,
The hard kind, worlds and inventions
The what-if variants of known laws.

Certainly not the enigmas of UFOs,
Crystal skulls, out-of-body experiences,
Parapsychology and mystic visions –
Fakes, hallucinations, faulty science
He would always declare, with nothing
Beyond what we sense and measure.

As for religions and life after death,
He'd studied holy books, saw social sense
In moral injunctions, but thought all else
A sop for minds too weak to cope
With what is here and that it ends.

When young he tried systems
Of self-improvement, was convinced
Only logic would cure the unknown,
And everyone should be shown this. Later
He returned to his tinkering with engines,
His plans for infinitely-variable gearboxes,
Which never left the drawing board,
Followed my interest in the paradoxes
Of light, gravity and quantum forces,
But laboured to fathom them,
Became a time and motion expert.

After his wife of over fifty years died,
He began using crystal pendulums
To contact her, announced he had
The healing touch, though no one felt
A thing, tried to read books on time
And consciousness, his glass of whisky
Always filled, no matter what the doctor said,
And sometime after lunch would settle
For diversions on TV, the mechanisms
Of DVDs and Cable far beyond him,
His vision winding down, winding down.

Black, with One White Spot

I had never seen death throes before.
Watched your body roll upwards a moment
And stretch, as if you had suddenly awakened
From one of those nightmares you used to have.

Thought you would snap back to endearing ways:
Drinking from the bowl with your left paw;
Nuzzling my face with whiskers so I'd awake
And feed you – done only minutes before.

You hopped down, seemed to collapse
And stumble, as if a leg had given way,
Then, so swiftly I wasn't sure if in play or pain,
You crabbed and rolled across the floor

To settle without a sound on your right side,
One gurgle-cry as I stroked and checked
For broken bones, kept stroking, waiting
For that purr we would hear across rooms.

I had never buried a pet before:
A hole in the front garden you haunted daily.
Your fur-riddled blanket. The brush always welcomed.
Food for your journey through darkness.

Wind ruffles roses on the grave.

Venture

What is it sprays ochre
Across hands laid upon ancient rock?

Fixes those shapes that resolve into stars
And the generations of planets?

Regards a perfect day
In the plume of dust a raindrop conceives?

Demands our delirium of knowing
And that incandescence ever after?

Man and Hunt

Never the next day without offerings
        to moon, to earth, to figures
        etched in imitation of herds
        or messengers between worlds
        words and gestures a charm
        for kill and homecoming

Never the hefted weapon without scalloped edge
        honed against spit and grazed stone
        eyes and muscles trained
        to measure arcs of intersection
        as bodies test speed, terrain
        lung ache, self-preservation

Never the toppling prey without silence
        in manoeuvres of decoy and trap
        without the prone sniffing of wind
        and fear, without spear-cast exhilaration
        without the dodge-seizure of thrashing limbs
        without the writhing and slowing spurt

Never the trussed meat without guilt
        at butchering this fellow creature
        without blood caught in palms
        a little for the earth, the rest
        drunk hot amongst cheers
        without the roasted share
        amongst all, the hero's portion
        the salted or smoked storage

Never the day ending without bowed awe

We Survivors

'There were gods for everything one might do' – Julian Jaynes,
The Origin of Consciousness in the Breakdown of the Bicameral Mind

Then came the time of wheeling voices.
We killed smiling foes because they told us to.
We razed cities because they said nothing.
The earth neglected its fields of grain.
Priests began listening to stone.

It was the time kings bound themselves with spies.
We invented laws to cope with silence.
We bent our knees to all things absent.
Armies drilled themselves towards slaughter.
Each generation decreed the next.

It was the time the grave startled us.
We burnt our best to summon direction.
We tracked the heavens for proof or hint.
Libraries stored our pleas and defections.
Songs reminded us of our deeds.

Then each mind listened to its echo.
We saw each world open in time.
We weighed each past with our dreams.
Words dart as sparks about the forge.
The last voices to question are our own.

Initiation

'O Unas, you have not departed dead, you have departed alive'
– Sarcophagus Chamber Texts, Pyramid of Unas

The ungilded lid seals him
To falcon-headed drumming
Echoing the stone chamber.

His breath quickens with the closing
Dark, the weaning air,
And slows into loamed faith

Won from scripture spells,
Theorems of the plumb line,
Elixirs of touch and laughter.

His body lightens as echoes
Sweep all talismans of memory
And thought into dismembered shadows,

Till nothing of risk remains
But hieroglyphs of breath,
Horizons of glittering wings.

Dolmen and Circle

Carrowmore Megalithic Cemetery, County Sligo, Ireland

when we came the gods themselves
scattered boulders across plains
and forests like falling stars
they glitter at dusk at dawn
some too heavy for one clan's
blessing we rolled them hauled them
layers of pebbles beneath them
as many as the beckoning stars
made of them shapes whispering
the world around within us
hollows and mountain bulges
cast and swept by the sun's rim
and the darkness under this
raised the biggest to observe
that place each life passes through
five boulders as three walls one
tilted on top sometimes more
pointing the way to sunrise
sometimes all covered by earth
mother and lover of each
we place our bones in bags stitched
from the skins of those we hunt
bury them in still corners
sing for moon sun stars passing
under the river-bright earth
seasons of meat shellfish fruit
leave the silent swirling dark
like a child blinking first light

stride the path till last light
strikes our eyes and once again
we gift our burnt bones to claim
water earth sky flame as breath

Newgrange Return

We wait beneath a beehive vault,
Layered stones without mortar,
Which has kept the chamber dry

And held the mound weight
Of two hundred thousand tons
For over six millennia.

We wait in darkness akin
To the enigma of those incisions
On kerbstones around the mound:

Spirals and triple spirals, circles within
Circles, lozenges, chevrons, wavy lines –
The serpentine passage narrowing light

To a thin beam creeping along the floor
Towards us, touching carved spirals
On the stone basin, widening

Into golden glow and afterglow,
Instant of world and winter hearths
Reborn to seed time and every harvest.

For a few seconds more, the utter
Darkness of waiting and faith,
Centre of suns about to open.

Scripture in the Round

Sacred, an exhibition at the British Library, September 2007

Somewhere outside, the addled cultures
Of exclusivity clash, and clash again,
As have all zealots, all purgers
Of scapegoats, all crusading armies,
To the same breathless end.

In here, Jew, Christian, Muslim,
The curious, the lapsed or distant,
Circle these Abrahamic accounts,
Variations on the one theme
Of listening to the source
Of all blessings.

We cannot touch the papyrus
Unearthed from the rubbish tip
Of ancient Oxyrhynchus, nor the gold
And vibrant ink letters and images
On vellum, the marriage contract,
The ceramic lamp – all transfigured
By the music of visionary tongues.

Can only stand before each
Torah, Gospel, Qur'an
As if before an opening star,
The heart thrumming with silence
We nourish outside.

Wu-Wei

'The Tao does nothing, and yet nothing is left undone' – Laozi

Here, nothing can save you
But verve, talent, training,
As you step to the line,
Bow to your opponent,

Take guard, await the start,
First feint, first strike, first block,
Gambits and manoeuvres
Of stance and flashing limbs,

The target a bare touch
Of skin, proof of control
And combat sense. Reason
Has no part, eye and thought

Too slow to second-guess
Each flurry attack, each
Sudden breach, fist and foot,
Ego and fear of blood,

A barrage of chess moves
With this mirror your foe.
Only reflex and faith
In a blank of self,

Raw channel of prowess,
Can parry and counter
The rote drills of violence
In nerve, muscle, will,

This ancient death rhythm
Made art, touchstone of self.
Someone scores, someone wins.
We bow to each other.

Letter to William Blake

Two hundred years on
And we're still not listening,
Even with the Age of Aquarius –
All that free love, those drugs
And rituals for raising
Consciousness – so that for most
The bear and bull of profit,
The spree of instant possessions,
The whiz-bang amusements
Of technology still hold sway.

Sometimes a seeker glimpses
What you saw every day –
The opening to Eden inside
A flower, the sun as a host
Of angels, the light of Imagination
Shining through the muck of Time,
Insights of truths far beyond
Those dark satanic mills
And the blood of innocents
Staining walls of Church and State.

Yet barely a few welcome death
As you did, singing your delight
At the unravelling of your body,
Hearing again the bee-sound of souls,
All tombs a womb into Eternity,
Place of energy and joy unchecked
By any rule except that of Vision –
And your great task of opening
Immortal Eyes, progress by contraries,
Still tigering our senses, our pride.

Climbing Glastonbury Tor

for Jo

The real magic is your reaching
The five-hundred-foot summit, crag-steps
Winding through drizzle, cleaving wind,

After standing beside me or in front,
After resting hands-to-knees or on a bench
As you drew on more faith-breath

And dared the dark maze of fear –
That memory-logic of you as a child
Climbing the steel tourist tower,

Legs slip-shooting through the gap
Between steps, dangle-scramble, grasp
By your mother before flailing drop…

You gasp-huddle in a corner
Of the stone chapel tower, never far
From weather wail and chill,

From that reeling aftertaste
Of all brinks contemplated,
All staircases hammer-pulse gripped.

I lean at compass-point edges,
Take photos of plummeting views
That later will jolt you into awe.

On the way down you clutch
My backpack, slide-shriek once or twice,
Shiver when precipice becomes ease.

Cows introduced for low greening
Crowd the thin path between trees
And ragged wet earth, will not move

Till you resort to that boom-tone
Of farmer voice learnt when young,
Slap rumps, clear a way as we laugh.

Legend says before death we will
Return to marvel more spiral dreams.
Your pulse, even now, ardent, more agile.

Weft

A spiderling stands on its head, casts
A lengthening line to snare a breeze,
Turns and clutches the silk kite,
Rides the temperature flux of air
To any gossamer horizon.

Design: Mt Ngungun

'Climb the mountains and get their good tidings' – John Muir

With vigour but far less breath than younger days
When such was a king-of-the-mountain race
Against fellow trampers of solitude, I scale
The steep, sun-grained watercourse
For a clearer distillation of design
Than the years before me have graced.

Each step towards the noonday summit drains
Vitality from blood, spasms my muscles
With lactic stings, draws sweat that films
The eye, until a well-met haven from glare:
A large cave inside bubble-burst basalt.

First, a libation soaking fine dust, a guzzle
While being chased by sentinel mosquitoes
From end to wind-pocked end then out,
But not before the gleaning of triangular,
Dark-faced wings anchored to solid shade,
Moth camouflage undone by quivering thorax.

Next, a little-used sidetrack to an edge where,
Far below, buzz saws and orchards endure, unwelcome
Except as touchstones of distance travelled, dispelled.

Raw sun razes the sparse foliage, returns me
To the wonder of signs: the black and yellow tail
Of a snake disappearing into undergrowth,
The blue-green butterfly bright in a helix of breeze,
The rust-red winged scarab darting onto rock.
Grit and sweat irritate creases of skin.

A spiderweb blocks one avenue through shade.
Distant engines drone like history. The moment
Drives through: foot to hollow filled with dust,
To worn edge, hand grasping the next tree for stability,
Coordination of body to eye – especially in sheer spaces
Where limbs move in rock-climber rhythm, three locked
To crevice or ledge, one spanning the new gap –
Until last heave of breath at the plateau near the pinnacle,
Where a spine of rocks shields me from the fulminating sun.

Here is space enough to wait for body to ease with air
And earth, the mind still questing for presence
And essence, mine or some elemental other,
Emblem of the ultimate, evidence of homecoming –
Then the whiff of some small animal's leavings
Along with my sweat, the obvious traffic of flies,
Bush brown, metallic green, those tiny scrambler ants
And bull leapers at their business of search and carry,
A grey-and-white skink basking for a moment,
Skittering when I shift for a better view
Of Regent Skippers, Wonder Browns,
Caper Whites, Blue Triangles
Spangling the thermals
In nuptial manoeuvres.

And beyond all this,
Dragonflies semaphore each other,
Then dive.

Looking for Grace

By definition it comes
When least expected. Yet we
Call for healing and vigour
When we are furthest from them,
Not knowing grace waits for us
To curse its absence, fall back
On faith, forget even that.

Then one day a host of birds
Blasts out of thick scrub, blue
Bodies, crimson wings blazing
Past blackened tree trunks, and we
Watch them embroider the sky.

The Dream Bird

Every dream flourishes from her throat,
Even the one in which she lies
Ulcerated and trembling
At the bottom of the wicker cage
You thought would protect her.

Feed her seeds soaked with honey
Bartered from the terrors and desires
Of your ordinary day. Fill her bowl
With water aerated in your lover's laughter.
Tell her those fears you wish to face
And those you have long forgotten.
Show her how clouds part
And the full moon tidals the blood.
Sit with her as she sleeps.

When she preens her crimson and gold
Feathers and her eyes reflect yours
Without tears, open your cage.
Let her pick you up in her talons.
Wait for the glory of the cold heights.
Give thanks for all songs as you fall,
For the bright scar of your return.

Homecoming

He savours the salt and sea spray one last time, turns into the tunnel. From high above rock, above sky, he watches himself walking into the dark, the tunnel always bending, sloping down, his footsteps sure. The air is dry, the wind behind him merging with the apple blossom breeze before him. He hears above him the beat-whoosh of wings and below him the rolling din of hooves, but sees nothing. His bare feet make no sound on rock. He walks, always noting the flow of air, flow of rock, flow of breath, his neck muscles twitching. Air presses on his naked skin.

Each step is heavy as he sees himself below the flow and genesis of rock. Each step, each breath, each vision of place is heavy for a moment, then gone. Each labour, each joy is heavy, then gone. Each vibrant and hesitant thought is heavy, then gone. He feels nothing but the flow of steps. He sees nothing but himself flowing into the spiral of tunnel, of dark, of breath that slows.

Then light that blinds and sharpens.

He stands on a cliff outcrop overlooking a deep valley of tall trees and gleaming rivers. He can see each leaf and ripple, carvings on distant mountains. He stretches his arms, bends his head back to gulp the high air. His tears taste of blood. Head still back, he feels the rapture and rupture of blood in the nostrils, ears, mouth, in the pores of his skin. He hears wingbeats, senses sentinel raptors land about him, feels beaks tear his skin. He stands, arms outstretched, and lets them feed. He screams, and the birds continue to feed.

Now he is curled on the rock and the totem beasts come for his organs, for the sinew of his muscles, for body fat. They growl, but he does not hear them. They snarl at each other and snap at the strictures of his flesh, but he does not feel them. His scream is long gone, and the only thing he sees as he watches from above is the seething mass of flesh and the white-flare of bones before they are broken for marrow, and he fades from watching.

Bone shards gleam as rain falls. White clouds reel along the valley floor. As it charges into the tunnel, the herd of wild horses pounds the shards to dust.

Wind whips and polishes the rock once more.

Above, Below

Like water, I surrender any time, any place
           to the songlines of the sun, and rise
           into the sky, only to plunge again.
Like water, the moon tugs me into
           flirtations of everything my waves lap
           and thread with thunder.
Like water, I conjure mist at dawn, at dusk,
           veiling and unveiling the land
           and all its diurnal broodings,
           so no one knows exactly what dreams
           approach, what missives dreams contain.
Like water, I seep into the most secret places
           and at length return with skeleton news
           of things hidden, ignored, forgotten,
           tinctures of jewels and mineral veins,
           echoes of slow-drip alabaster ornaments.
Like water, each drop of me contains all
           of me, each drop spreads itself over
           all surfaces, reflecting the shimmer-pulse
           of any seam of light, and each drop, under
           ferment of heat and pressure, custom
           of gravity, shapes itself to a sphere,
           to a teardrop, into searing ice or steam,
           toil and comfort of snow and rain.
Like water, I flow to the lowest point, path
           of most doubt, cracking open rock,
           carving vistas, flooding plains, greening
           deserts, glossing wings and leaves.

Like water, nothing can stop me, everything
        drinks of me, everything bleeds with me.
Like water, where I am not, life is not.
Like water, where I am scattered, words and touch burst free.

Contact

Maybe it had to do with imagination
Spiced by a heartburn mélange of red wine,
Garlic mushroom, grilled Orange Roughy.

By three hours watching Sagan's heroine wormhole
Her way to a covenant of faith beyond paradigms.
By five previous weeks decoding perennial texts

For spiral insights. By a lifetime of feather meditations
On connect-a-dot reality, its pulsations of negative space.
And the undreamt, unsought spray of light beyond

The bedroom door, where there should be none,
Vanished a moment later. There was no sleep,
Nothing but moonlight gloss on tallboy, bookcase,

Speckling on the door's edge. Nothing but the weight
Of changing weather creaking walls and ceiling. Nothing
But the enticement of my lover's warmth under the doona.

Then a sudden kink in this flow of perception,
Stage lights clicked off in a deepening cube of black.
A turning without eye movement, a sense of all negation

Of breath, nothing to touch, nothing to generate touch,
Just a prickling presence outside me, yet deep inside my core
Of awareness, something from before memory rekindling

Memory and grasp. I spoke my surprise, affirmation, conclusion.
Found everything returned to moonlight. Regretted my fondness
For analysis. Fell asleep awaiting more from the heaving dark.

This Enterprise of Dust

By the time you read this
At least 50,000 cells
Of your body will die.

And with each person met
We handshake cells,
Mix and match electrons
That swarm about us.

So that everyone, everything
On this planet renders
The other through at most
Seven trades of touch.

And when we die, after
So many seven-year cycles
Of new cells, new electrons,
Same pivot of mind and memory,

The planet reclaims us,
With all those folded-in lives
Of labourer and sage,
Insect and blossom,

And our children's children
Will share and shed us,

Until winds and magnetic currents
Fling us into further orbits
Of planets, stars, black holes.

Palette

'The most beautiful thing we can experience is the mysterious'
– Albert Einstein

Just as we do with clouds
We see nebulae as shapes and designs,
Name them in the familiar –

Helix, Boomerang, Red Rectangle,
Tarantula, Butterfly, Eagle,
Hourglass, Cat's Eye, Rosette –

Such swirls, veils, ripple-bursts of energy,
Incandescent pillars, Catherine wheels,
Flickering lattices, florid spumes,

Chameleon whirlpools of wavelengths
Captured and composed with colour:
Orange for starlight, blue for dust,

Green for hot gases, red for hot light,
Furnaces of radiation and matter,
Cosmic Rorschach tests, mirages

Of galaxies, planets, moons, life itself
Woven into and out of existence
Millennia before we and our machines

Could trap their scattered signals,
Seek to unravel their snakeskin fate,
Keep naming in the face of absence.

How We Come to Touch

From the midpoint of nothing rapping on nothing
From the tumble-burst of light out of nothing
From light folding light into point, curve, mass and law
From mass splitting and blooming, dust swirling into weight
        into those contractions that become star and planet
From earth and ocean, from sky, from pulses of lightning between
From one cell to many, hunter to prey, fin to leg
        and the opposable thumb
From amoeba division to gender genesis
From that moment gaze locks with gaze
        and our enterprise of joy
        is the other's joy
From all moments we dare the stun-blossom
        of a mouth that hovers over our mouth
        and breathes our name
From nuzzle into nape of neck to slide of tongue
From every time skin opens to whimper of skin
From the double spiral of spines
From the revolving constellations of breath
From the rushing pulse of caress and arch
        senses honed to the prism
        of light thrilling light
From the air thrumming
        with the soft blaze of our bodies
From the way we breathe echoes of silence
        to one another
        as time spirals out again

From all this to all this
As we embrace the nothing
      between us
And the nothing
      that becomes us

Lemniscate

To fathom the fact of one
Added to itself without
End, we conceive a symbol,
An eight on its side, only
Digit that closes itself,
Except that touchstone zero,
Though Buddhist images show
Prayer beads – a circle – twisted
In the middle – figure eight.

Whether or not a Big Crunch
Inevitably follows
A Big Bang, we believe in
Never-ending life, even
If our own begins and ends
With the briefest cosmic wink.

Yet in that time we are clouds,
Creatures that when magnified
Bare the same structure, again
And again, as we go deeper,
Finer, fractal holograms
Echoing the universe.

So I gaze into your eyes,
See brown and blue reflected
Again and again, finer,
Deeper, till one of us blinks
And we laugh, glossy pupils
Falling into each other.

This Charge Between Us

That cloud of radiant musk
In rooms of skin rhythms
Like the moon-renewing sea

In rooms of glistening silence
After stunned and blessèd cries
In rooms of hands outstretched

To the quivering other, fanning
The cloud's rising exaltation
Of mouth and tongue seeking out

The ever-rushing, nourishing dark
Each room inside us and outside
Quickening with scintillations and scent

As when fields of kneeling flowers
Face again the sun after eclipse
As when a nimbus of birds

Bursts one horizon to another
As when we see through deep
Whirlwinds of chanting flesh

Our single grin of recognition
As at our first touch, first sigh
And every glance afterwards

Spanish Bluebells

Since midwinter,
As with each year lately,
We've craved like children
That clamour of colour.

At first, only muzzled earth
Round the wind-grey persimmon tree.

Then, cusp of season downpours
Forge green eruptions of strap-leaves,
Prime sudden slim towers
Of knotted dark blue buds.

Soon after, the scripted sun
Peels away the buds to hang parabolic
From swinging stalks, to unfurl into
Six-petal variations of flare and shade,
Each with dark stamen-clappers,
Royal blue pinstripes and crowns,
Lavender sound-bow walls –
Such bell-ruffles of profusion,
Few and resonant weeks.

Before decay into ragged stalks,
Counterpoint bulbs,
Strike tone and after-hum.

Moments after Meditation

Somewhere else car bombs split-screen the news
Somewhere else couples harangue vows and baggaged fears
Somewhere else children mimic fashion of what works   what conceals

And here   sometime else   rifles colonise   ploughs desecrate
        theodolites divide   motor pools accumulate

Here also   but now   with sun and wind circulating their blessing
        with black birds snacking in the vegie patch next door
        with one daisy nodding its petalled banner
    to no one in particular

Silence infuses skin and thought   earth and couch grass

Much like that pause
        before
                a newborn's first surprise
                      of light

Much like that link
        when lovers rock
                their masks of touch
                      into arch

Much like that gasp
        of last surprise
                eyes opening
                      a deeper hue

Our leap into all stories, all landscapes, at once

Naming Instinct

Sligo, Ireland, August 2009

Not knowing its name, my being
On a far-flung island, its creatures
Known only by reputation,

I have no choice but to listen:
High-pitched chioo, chioo, chioo, or
Queeka, queeka, queeka, almost the sound

Of worn brakes jabbed to slow down,
Or a thin bronze staff tapped against oak
To call ancestors to dark clearings.

Not knowing what it looks like –
Midnight, the bird bounding
From one branch to the next,

Behind a maze of branches, calling
To mate, to mark territory, to state
Its own being-bliss – I imagine it

Brindled, slim-bodied, tawny-flecked neck,
Oil-gloss eyes that scan always,
Its red beak open, with each note

Chiming leaves and balmy air, all ears,
Etymologies of breath behind its eyes.
It knows nothing of thresholds.

Not knowing what to do next, I stop
Wondering, stop straining to charm the bird
And its rustling, moon-riddled tree,

Open gaze and hearing to whatever waits
Beyond the imprints and echoes of words,
The swing of breath and song, the poise.

Summer Adepts

With a recent shift in boundaries
Our backyard acquired an apple tree,
Though we were one day late for the harvest.

A bevy of rainbow lorikeets,
Never seen before
In all our seven years here,

Chatter like children at a birthday party
As they gorge themselves on the dense flesh
And acrid juice under the skin of crab apples.

They are welcome, their skeins of delight
As they dart about the tree an evocation
Of every joy issued from the throats

Of all their ancestors and descendants,
Millennia of dinosaurs, unborn fledglings.
Much the same as the palette of their livery

Draws out the traces of every landscape
They have ventured through, and will:
Their blue masks like the near-dusk glaze

Of lake water. The red, orange, yellow
Splashes at beak, eye, chest and underwings
Like baked rock, lightning-torched grass plains.

Their green body stockings and upper wings,
The succulences of all their foragings
At fruit and leaf. Their cries are thanks.

Their cries are companionship. Their cries
Crescendo and echo long after bodies fall
From the treetops of other seasons, long after

No one remains to remember them, long after
Nothing remains but the last lightning,
Its flash and crack and flickering silence.

Little Wattlebird

When I open the front door
He has arrived at last,
Swinging on the telephone wire
Above the pink camellia bush.

After each May Day, whenever
Buds goosebump its branches,
I await his appearance, gold-winged,
Advance scout for a family

Come to breed
Generation after generation,
This bush their nest barricade,
Their nectar restaurant.

And each day he broadcasts
Any one of nine sounds –
The soft throaty *Yekkop yekkop*,
That *shnairt!* of alarm,

Those squeaky trill-flourishes –
Here I am, Keep clear,
This is mine, The sun is shining –
Often rousing us to our day,

His and theirs already started:
Build a nest, feed a family,
Teach fledglings to trust feathers,
Perch on wire or branch, watching,

Till the nectar runs dry,
The weather changes tune,
The fledglings preen for mating –
Time come for nomads to criss-cross

Latitudes and longitudes,
Navigating by star, by magnetic field,
By tang of air and moisture,
Wingtips angling towards sunset,

Ancestral flight paths forever looping
Back to old haunts, new blossoms.
And a door somewhere creaks with welcome,
Generation to generation.

Climbing the Tree

'All truths wait in all things' – Walt Whitman, *Song of Myself*

At first you are a cautious climber, moving
Only one limb at a time, testing
The bearing of each branch, pausing at
Each sign of muscle twitch, resting often
To consider every possible fall,
The impossibility of retreat, resisting
Always the burden of broken skin,
Intolerance of pulled muscles.
Soon you are stretching further, judging
Grip of weight and accustomed reflex,
Trusting gaps with the grace of muscle,
Climbing further, faster, with easy breath,
Enjoying the sway of branches as you sway.

One day you reach the highest junction
And sweep a glance of all possible moments –
From the pause of a spider on fractured bark
To the sudden wingbeat above you.
From the silent crouch of your horizon
To the edge of a faint moon sifting nightfall.
From the gasp of joggers and cyclists
On the concrete perimeter of the river
To the pealing of distant church bells.

That day, or another, a storm will dare you,
And you will ponder the glamour of lightning,
Raindrops coincident with welcomed sweat,
Before you descend to gather your days.

Yet day after day it is never the same tree:
Always the split and broken boundaries of branches
And the slow accretion of living wood about the dead.
One day you will note the circus mass of spiders
Hatched into tree-fold and the wind's tremor of web.
Two days later, when only silken shreds remain,
You ponder the fates of predator and prey.

And each time you notice the way your back eases
Into the veins of bark as you regard the span
Of leaf, of branch and their embracing gaps,
Knowing one day you will never leave here.

Kondalilla Falls

Easter holidays, 2011

1

After a thousand steps past palm trees,
Tallowwood trees, strangler figs, elkhorns,
Staghorns, rotting logs, metre-high seedlings,

When you step onto the expanse
Of moist, moss-patched striated rock,
The unseasonal downpour has stopped.

You find a suitable seat near the cable barrier.
Remove hat, jacket, shoes and socks.
Ignore the rising damp of your pants.

Ignore too the tourists, with their kids
Who screech at the long-limbed spider
And try to stomp on it.

Shut out the local lads hooting
As they dive-bomb the waterhole behind you –
When one leaps, the other takes a photo.

Watch the red-bodied, hand-span dragonfly
Perch at the edge of a small rock pool,
Twitch its wings occasionally and wait

Possibly for the three tiny tadpoles
That soon appear and dart the surface
With ripples as they chase each other.

Follow the yellow butterfly towards
The rumbling white and brown ribboned water
Tumbling over the lip of the falls, to plunge

Ninety vertical metres. Feel if you can
Through the soles of your feet the thrumming
Of this quickening water, the mountain quivering.

Stare across the expanse of gorge and valleys,
The hills covered in cascades of rainforest,
No breath of wind to stir the mottled greens.

Breathe slowly. Look closer at nearby trees,
Their leaves glazed by sunlight's keenness
Through over-taut clouds. When you flick off

The tiny leech stinging your right foot,
It's time to put on your gear,
Brush down your pants, head towards

The bottom of the falls, to feel,
Barefoot or not, the white-noise thunder
As tons of water pummel water and rock.

2

The frenzy of rushing waters
So pounds your hearing
Only sight remains.

The voluminous plumes,
The abrupt explosions,
The plummets and swirls

Become minute variations
Of contour and mass,
Flux and constancy,

The same carousel
Of liquid, the diverse
Circuitries of time –

Like the flame inflections
In a fireplace,
Like the poise and beat

Of blood and breath,
As skin of the world
Ripples, opens

The Decree of All Dreams

'What land is native to us but a dream
We have told one another, leaf by leaf'
– Kathleen Raine, 'The Dream'

What do you see in dreams you cannot remember when you awake? Could it be the vision your childhood invoked in the backyard, under the tree, the night the moon linked arms with a star and another star swerved in flight, when the dog howled for a moment and the cat nuzzled your chin to keep you awake, to demand a scratch behind its left ear, its purring so loud you wondered whether the neighbours would hear or the stars would echo? Would you escape there if you could, not remembering the way, not recalling the exact boundaries of that place or the parameters of movement there? If you could remember that dream, would you tell it to another or keep it the sacred myth your amnesia guarantees for you but which also tempts you?

There is a dark forest somewhere you once visited, somewhere beyond the thicket of tall grass from which flows that raw water you love to drink but have forgotten why. That water dances in your mouth and throat, cools the rage of compulsion earth years have schooled into you. That water shocks the face into recognition, the eyes into focus, flares your nostrils as you strive to embrace the essence of mist above the stream. That water is the flood of all dreams if you but allow it, and you know that somewhere through that matted mass of razor grass and spiny bush ahead of you, as you crawl on hands and knees and, later, on your stomach, there is the fountain from which you will drink the remembrance of all your dreams and, beyond that fountain, the vivid landscape over which you will reign with a simple walk, touching each rock, bush and tree, touching each animal as it comes to you, counting those others who go about their simple business, naming, if you like, though it will only be a remembering of something someone may have done and which nobody considers worthwhile here. You will meet everyone who has travelled this way before, everyone who will travel this way, and be amazed as you sit down with them by a campfire to talk, or lie on your back eating blackberries and gazing at the marvel and question of clouds. You will continue your way to the edge of your domain, where there is nothing but the fear of nothing. Once there, you will take three deep breaths and, once more, jump…

Summer Walk, Early

To be so close
Yet still not there –
On a path strewn

With dead leaves
No movement
But a green-gold fly

In a maze of wings
No sound
But my thoughts

On what may shift
If I wait long enough
Let breath hover

Let words disappear
Forget the path
Twisting up the far slope

Be so empty
The forest opens
With revels of light

And when I breathe
I carry it with me

Leave myself there

Acknowledgements

Grateful acknowledgment is made to the following publications, in which poems in this book first appeared, sometimes in a different form: *Australian Poetry Members Anthology, Avant, Azuria, Blue Dog, Divan, Eureka Street, Mascara Literary Review, Muse Apprentice Guild* (USA), *papertiger, Pendulum, Plumwood Mountain, Poetry d'Amour* 2013, *Rabbit, Said the Rat!, Stars Like Sand: Australian Speculative Poetry, Temenos Academy Review* (UK), *The Paradise Anthology, Yeats 150*.

'Fall Out' won the 2005 Melbourne Poets Union International Poetry Competition; 'Tawny Frogmouth' was shortlisted for the 2008 Rosemary Dobson Prize; 'Easeful Death' was Commended in the Eastern Regional Libraries 2009 National Poetry Writing Competition; and 'Above, Below' was shortlisted for the Blake Poetry Award 2010.

I would like to thank Veronica Calarco, founder of Stiwdio Maelor in Wales, for providing a quiet yet stimulating environment for artists and writers. During my three residencies there, I enjoyed insightful conversations about art, literature, language and landscape with Veronica and my fellow residents, which aided my work on this manuscript as well as on other ongoing projects.

I would also like to acknowledge Catherine Bateson, Nick Engelman, Ray Liversidge, Robyn Rowland and the late Max Richards for their help during the preparation of this work, and John Jenkins and Alex Skovron for their astute editorial suggestions.

Finally, and most especially, I would like to thank my wife, Jo, for her advice, encouragement, support, and the ever-reliable scribbles of her red pen.

www.ingramcontent.com/pod-product-compliance
Lightning Source LLC
Chambersburg PA
CBHW070050120526
44589CB00034B/1709